WHO WAS MICHAEL FARADAY?

Biography Books Best Sellers
Children's Biography Books

BABY PROFESSOR

EDUCATION KIDS

Speedy Publishing LLC

40 E. Main St. #1156

Newark, DE 19711

www.speedypublishing.com

Copyright 2017

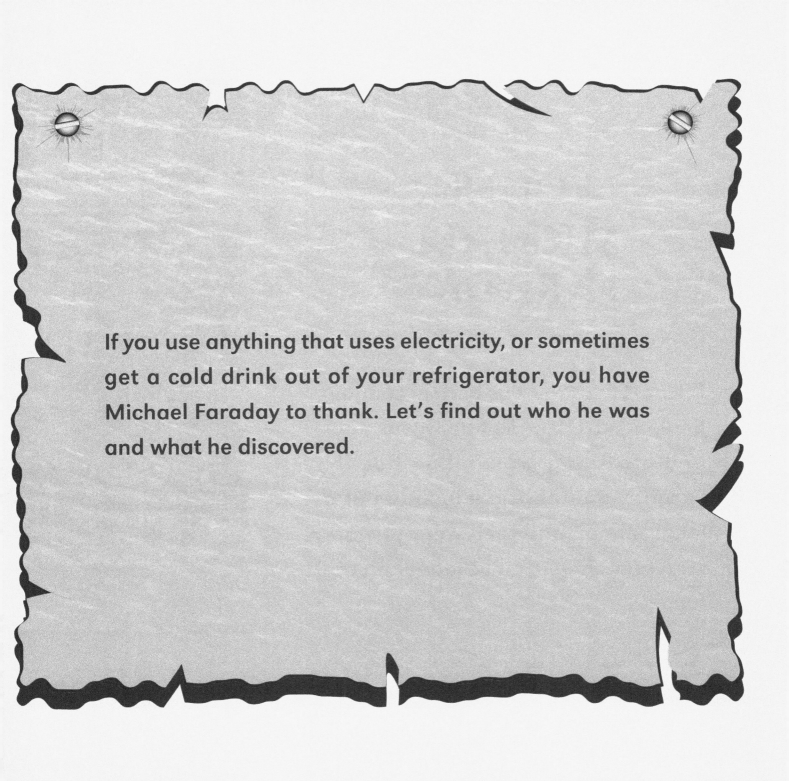

If you use anything that uses electricity, or sometimes get a cold drink out of your refrigerator, you have Michael Faraday to thank. Let's find out who he was and what he discovered.

YOUNG MICHAEL FARADAY

Michael Faraday was born in London, England in 1791. His family was poor and his father was in bad health. Faraday got a basic education at a local school, and then went to work for a bookshop to make money for the family.

MICHAEL FARADAY

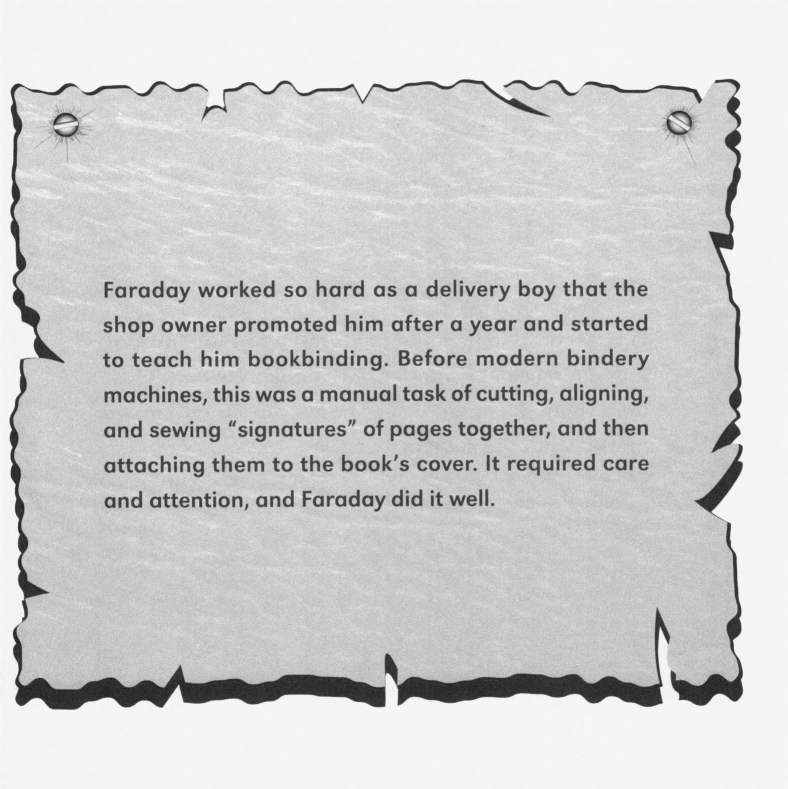

Faraday worked so hard as a delivery boy that the shop owner promoted him after a year and started to teach him bookbinding. Before modern bindery machines, this was a manual task of cutting, aligning, and sewing "signatures" of pages together, and then attaching them to the book's cover. It required care and attention, and Faraday did it well.

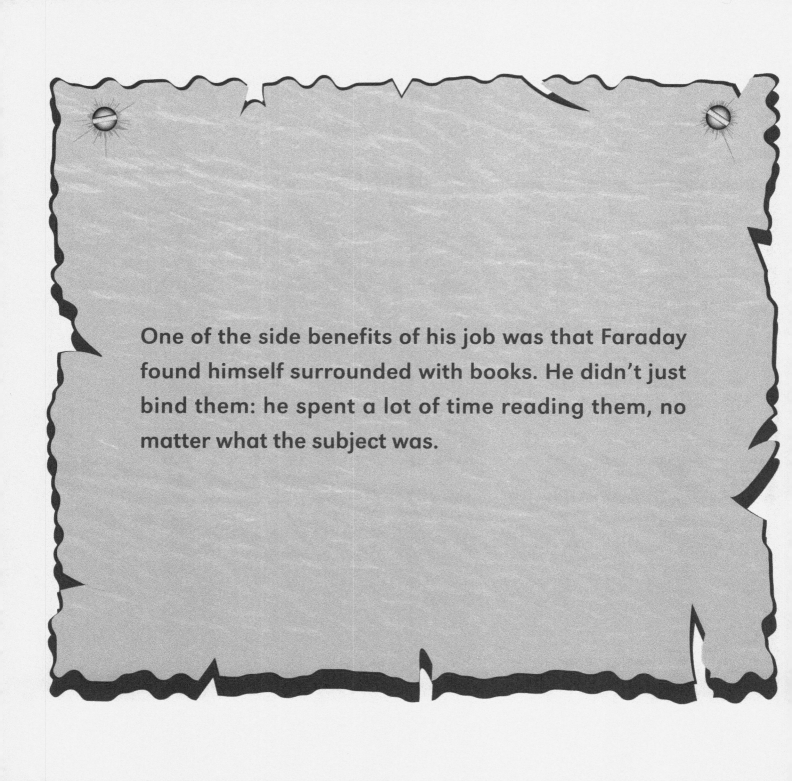

One of the side benefits of his job was that Faraday found himself surrounded with books. He didn't just bind them: he spent a lot of time reading them, no matter what the subject was.

MICHAEL FARADAY

DISCOVERING SCIENCE

After a while, Faraday began to focus on reading books about science. He started spending some of what little money he had on chemicals and equipment so he could work out for himself some of the things he was reading about.

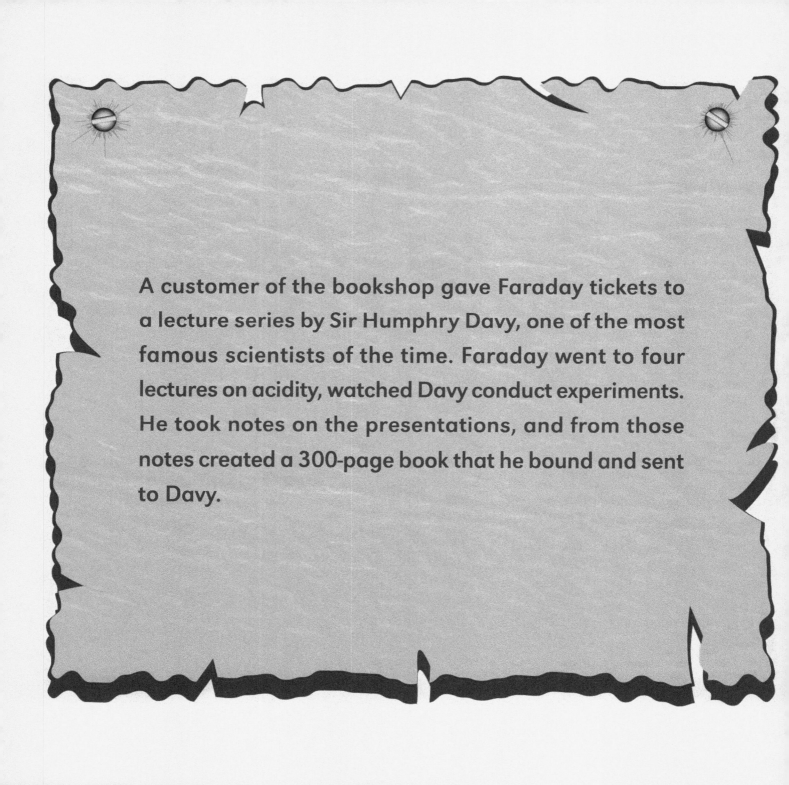

A customer of the bookshop gave Faraday tickets to a lecture series by Sir Humphry Davy, one of the most famous scientists of the time. Faraday went to four lectures on acidity, watched Davy conduct experiments. He took notes on the presentations, and from those notes created a 300-page book that he bound and sent to Davy.

HUMPHRY DAVY

THE ROYAL INSTITUTION

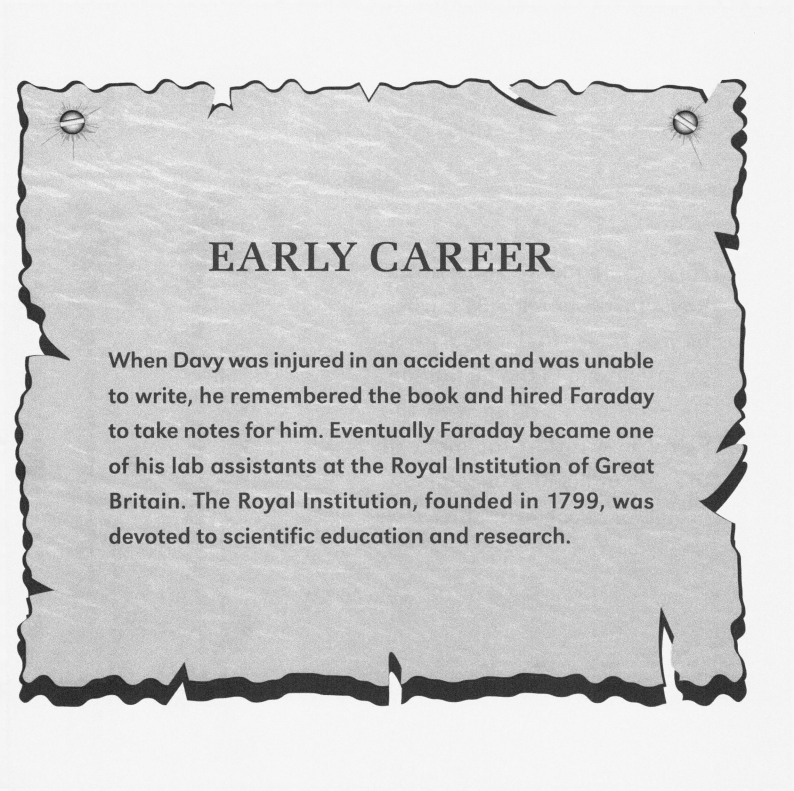

EARLY CAREER

When Davy was injured in an accident and was unable to write, he remembered the book and hired Faraday to take notes for him. Eventually Faraday became one of his lab assistants at the Royal Institution of Great Britain. The Royal Institution, founded in 1799, was devoted to scientific education and research.

Faraday began his work at the Royal Institution in 1813, when he was 21. He had a salary and an attic room in the Institution. He went on working with the Royal Institution for most of the rest of his life, becoming a professor of chemistry there.

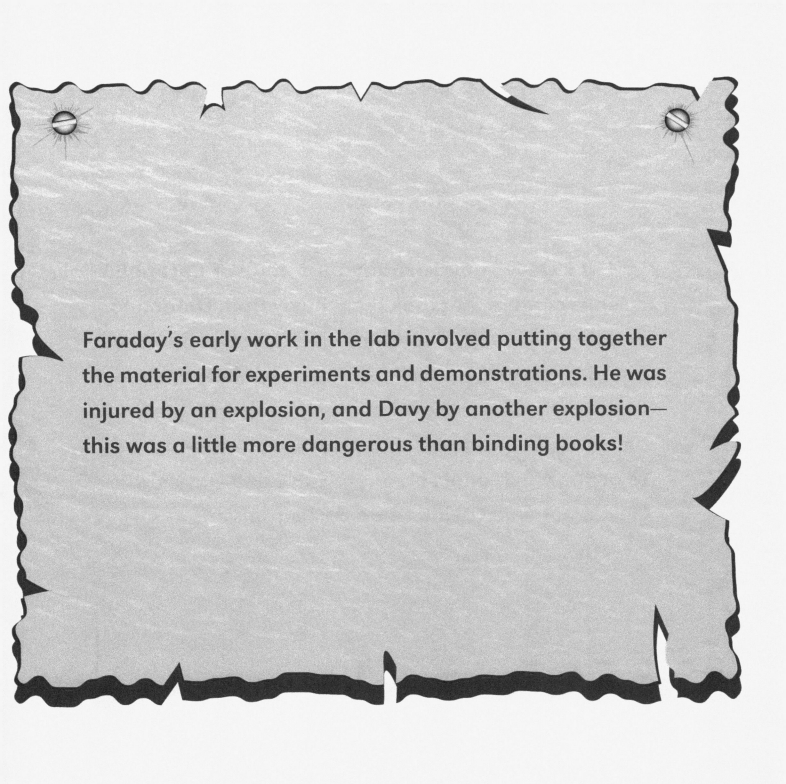

Faraday's early work in the lab involved putting together the material for experiments and demonstrations. He was injured by an explosion, and Davy by another explosion—this was a little more dangerous than binding books!

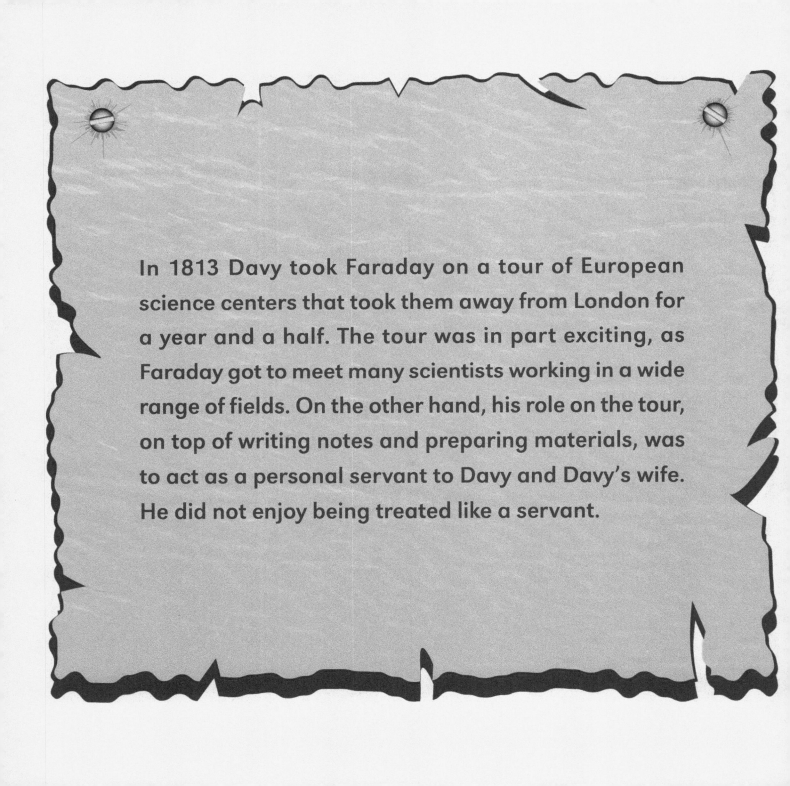

In 1813 Davy took Faraday on a tour of European science centers that took them away from London for a year and a half. The tour was in part exciting, as Faraday got to meet many scientists working in a wide range of fields. On the other hand, his role on the tour, on top of writing notes and preparing materials, was to act as a personal servant to Davy and Davy's wife. He did not enjoy being treated like a servant.

MICHAEL FARADAY

MICHAEL FARADAY

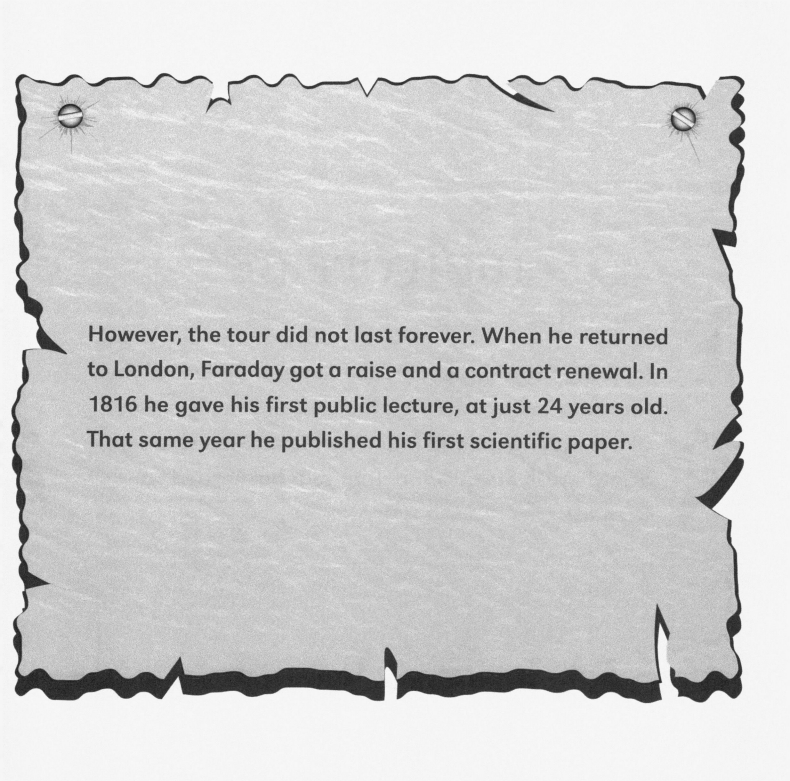

However, the tour did not last forever. When he returned to London, Faraday got a raise and a contract renewal. In 1816 he gave his first public lecture, at just 24 years old. That same year he published his first scientific paper.

HIGH OFFICE

In 1821, Faraday became the Superintendent of the laboratories of the Royal Institution. He moved out of the attic room and into a comfortable apartment elsewhere in the building. That year he married Sarah Bernard.

THE ROYAL INSTITUTION LABORATORY

ROYAL SOCIETY

Faraday was elected to the Royal Society in 1824, when he was 32. The Royal Society was founded in 1660, and gathered the most important scientists and researchers into regular meetings to learn from each other. This was a high honor and showed that the greatest scientists of the period recognized the importance of Faraday's work. Later he was twice invited to become president of the Royal Society, but he turned down the honor both times.

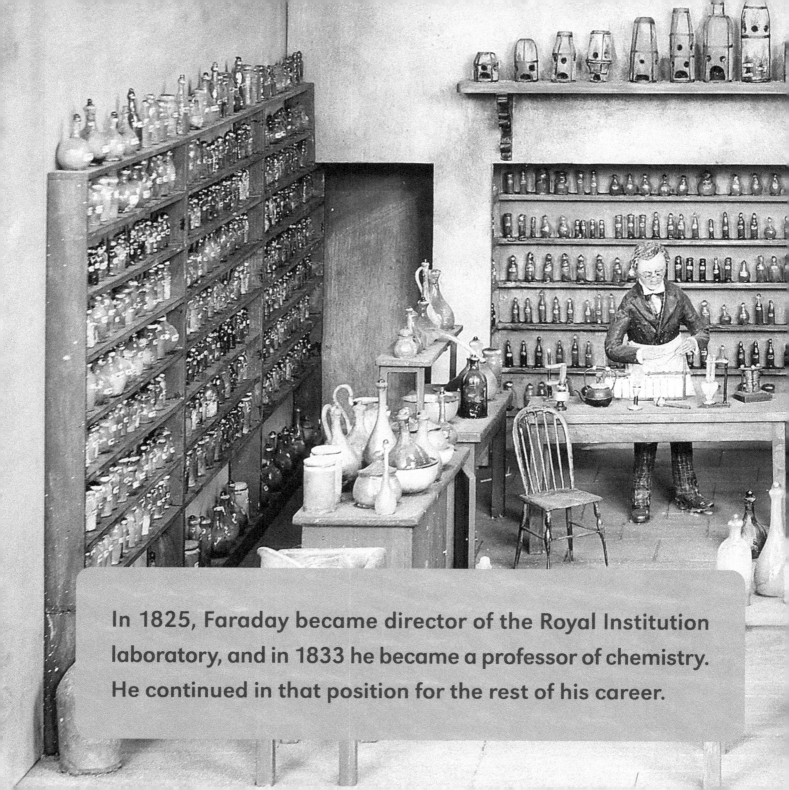

In 1825, Faraday became director of the Royal Institution laboratory, and in 1833 he became a professor of chemistry. He continued in that position for the rest of his career.

FARADAY'S LABORATORY AT THE ROYAL INSTITUTION

Here are some of
Michael Faraday's important discoveries.

ELECTRIC MOTOR

ELECTROMAGNETIC ROTATION (1821)

Faraday worked with the idea, first discovered by Hans Christian Oersted, that a wire carrying an electric current could have magnetic properties. Faraday showed that electricity would flow through a wire if a varying magnetic field was applied to it. You can create a varying magnetic field by simply passing a horseshoe-shaped magnet over a wire. The magnet has positive and negative ends, and they produce a varying magnetic field in the wire. Faraday demonstrated that variation of a magnetic field could produce electricity.

Applying this principle creates most of the power we use in our homes. A power plant burns fuel of some kind to turn a turbine which has many wrapped bundles of wires inside a huge electromagnet, and the turning creates electricity!

JOHN DALTON

LIQUID GAS (1823)

Faraday confirmed a theory put forward by John Dalton that all gases could be turned to liquids with a combination of low temperatures and high pressure. Faraday was able to turn chlorine and ammonia into liquids for the first time. He also demonstrated how to return gases to their original state through a controlled process that transfers the low temperature to other material.

Faraday's discovery is the basis for the cooling functions we use in refrigerators and air conditioners. Ferdinand Carré used Faraday's discovery in 1862 to demonstrate the first ice-making machine designed for general use. The machine could produce 200 kilograms of ice in an hour, using ammonia as the coolant in the system.

BENZENE MOLECULES

BENZENE (1825)

In 1825, Faraday discovered benzene in the oily waste material resulting from using gas for street lights in London. This was a very important step in chemists understanding chemical bonding.

FARADAY'S LAWS OF ELECTROLYSIS (1834)

Electrochemistry studies what happens when an electrode is in contact with an ionic substance, and electricity passes through the electrode. This field of study led to the creation of the lithium-ion and metal hydride batteries which are essential to devices like mobile phones. Faraday outlined the laws that govern what happens to substances in these conditions, based on his observations.

THE FARADAY CAGE
(1836)

Faraday discovered that, if you make room or a cage out of metal and apply an electric charge to it, the charge is basically on the outside of the framework. If you conduct an experiment inside a Faraday Cage, it will not be influenced by electrical activity outside of the cage. A modern application of this discovery is that mobile communications are blocked by a Faraday Cage, including listening devices and similar spy tools.

Light Beam

Unpolarized Light

Faraday established a relationship between light and electromagnetic energy. This led to James Maxwell's proof, in 1864, that light itself can be considered an electromagnetic wave. Faraday's discovery related to the effect a magnetic field has on the polarization of a beam of light.

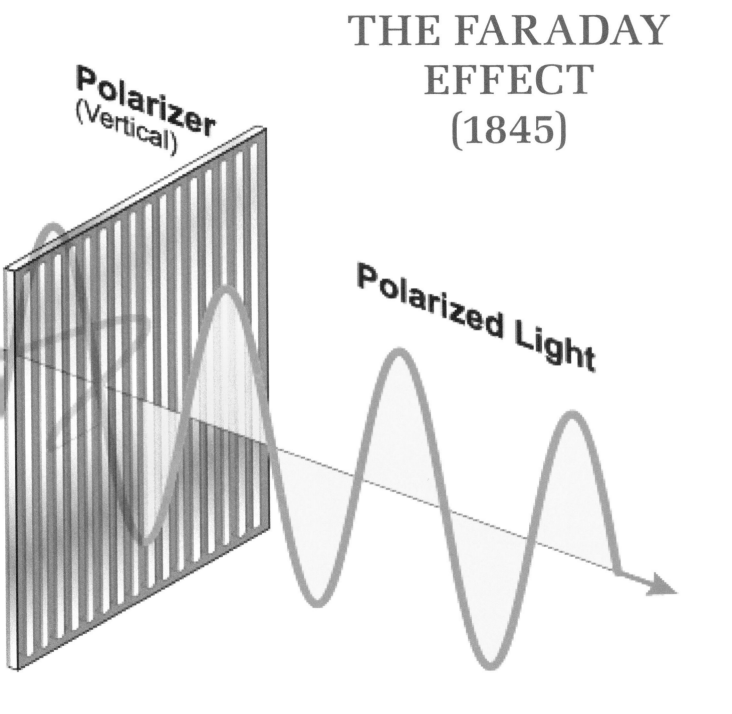

THE FARADAY EFFECT (1845)

Polarizer (Vertical)

Polarized Light

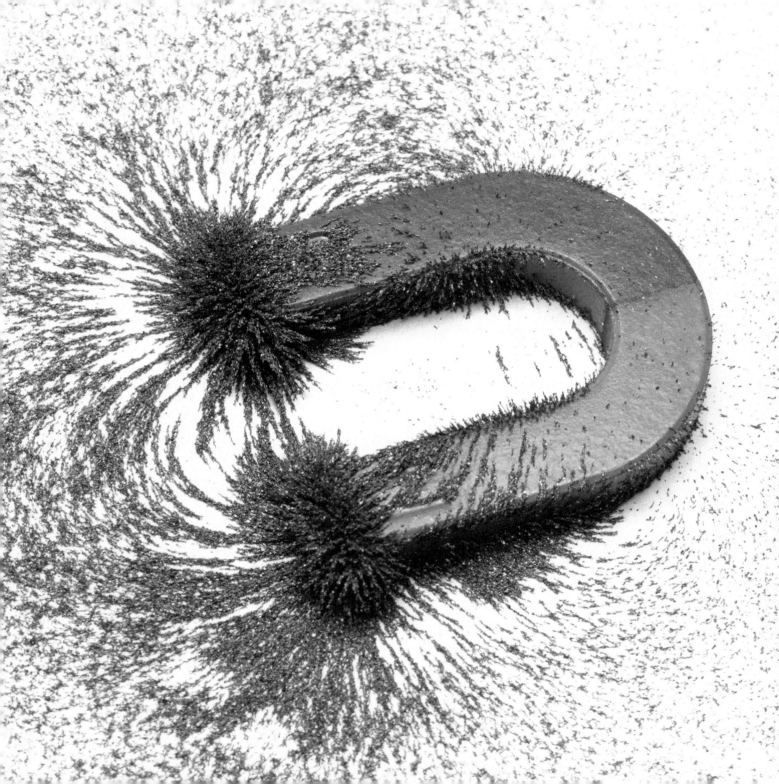

DIAMAGNETISM (1845)

Everyday magnets show ferromagnetism: anything with iron in it will respond to a magnet, and can even be turned into a magnet. Faraday showed that all substances, not just those with iron in them, are "diamagnetic". Diamagnetism pushes away from a positive magnetic charge.

Most objects are very weakly diamagnetic, but the force holds interesting possibilities. For example, a living creature like a frog has a certain amount of diamagnetism. If you apply the correct magnetic field to the frog, you should be able to make it levitate, or hover in the air!

DIAMAGNETISM

In Faraday's time this discovery was only of theoretical interest. Modern research is showing practical uses of diamagnetism. For instance, if you can make a vehicle hover slightly above the rails that guide it, you can reduce the friction between the two to almost zero. This would greatly reduce the amount of energy you need to move the vehicle.

LAST YEARS

Michael Faraday's health was never strong, and in the 1840s he became less and less well. He was able to do less research. He was given housing at Hampton Court, a royal residence, in honor of his scientific achievements, and he died there in 1867 at the age of 75.

WESTMINSTER ABBEY

As he was drawing near the end of his life, the government offered to provide burial space for Faraday in Westminster Abbey, where kings, queens, and great scientists like Isaac Newton were buried. Faraday declined the honor.

WHAT HOLDS YOU BACK?

Michael Faraday began in a poor situation, and was never in the best of health. But he devoted all the skills, energy and curiosity he had to discovering new things. He was known to keep following his hunches until he could either prove or disprove them scientifically. Most of the time his hunch turned out to be correct.

MICHAEL FARADAY

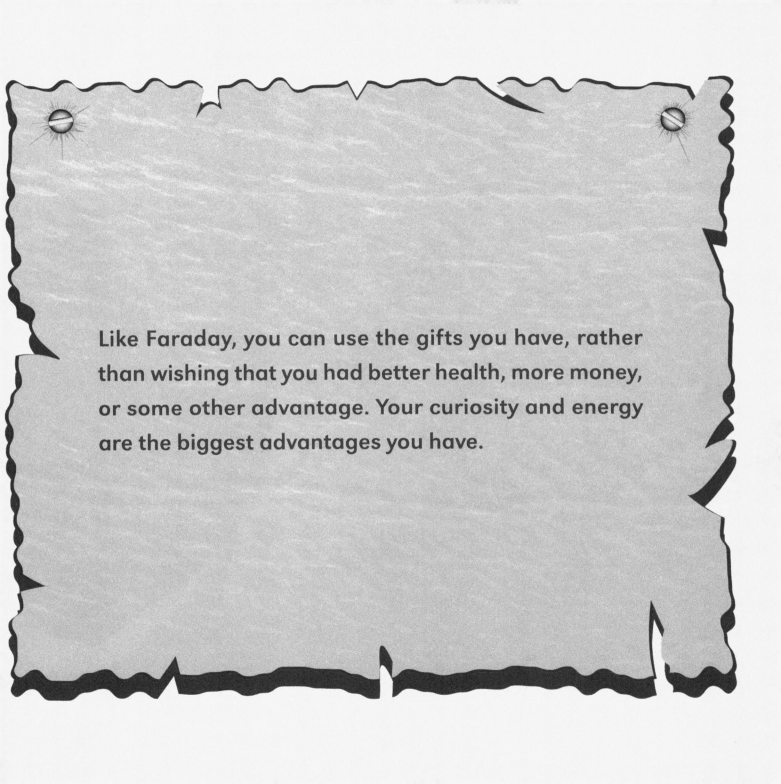

Like Faraday, you can use the gifts you have, rather than wishing that you had better health, more money, or some other advantage. Your curiosity and energy are the biggest advantages you have.

To learn about other people who did not let their limitations hold them back, read Baby Professor books like A Rich Man in Poor Clothes: The Story of St. Francis of Assisi and I Got it From My Mama! Gregor Mendel Explains Heredity.

Visit

BABY PROFESSOR
EDUCATION KIDS

www.BabyProfessorBooks.com

to download Free Baby Professor eBooks
and view our catalog of new and exciting
Children's Books

CPSIA information can be obtained
at www.ICGtesting.com
Printed in the USA
BVHW022127151222
654222BV00009B/755